SUMMARY

THE SUBTLE ART OF NOT GIVING A F*CK

A COUNTERINTUITIVE APPROACH TO LIVING A GOOD LIFE

by Mark Manson

Proudly Brought to you by
OneHour Reads

Table of Contents

EXECUTIVE SUMMARY

In *"The Subtle Art of Not Giving A F*ck: A Counterintuitive Approach to Living a Good Life"*, Mark Manson follows the road not taken by presenting a set of seemingly weird tactics to living a good life. His ultimate proposition is that people need to start caring less about everything. Instead, the key to living a good life is in individuals knowing what matters to them and not wasting energy stressing over every little thing. He then proceeds to educate us on how to move forward by going backward.

Manson strongly believes that the endless pursuit of a flawless life, fueled by today's picture-perfect social media standards, is responsible for many of the psychological illnesses that have become rampant. The book culminates in a conclusion that we need to look beyond ourselves, drop the entitled airs, and embrace the ugliness and uncertainties before we can live better lives.

Manson sometimes delivers his wisdom in a graphic language that may put readers off at first. Once you can get past that, however, there is a wealth of practical insight delivered in an easy-to-understand style. Not only does he not give conventional advice, he also does not write conventionally.

The title is definitely not the only shocking thing about this book but, love it or hate it, Mark Manson's book is not one to be forgotten in a hurry.

CHAPTER 1: DON'T TRY

Key Takeaways:

- *Most motivational and self-help materials do more harm than good because they fix your gaze on what you don't have*
- *Becoming a better person is not synonymous with becoming successful*
- *Obsessively pursuing adequacy is a sign of inadequacy and dissatisfaction*
- *Discomfort is only natural. Trying to avoid it at all costs is what is harmful*
- *Stressing over everything is a sign that you've got nothing significant to use your 'stress' on*
- *Stop giving a hoot about everything!*

Your poster boy for a motivational figure is not likely to be a broke, gambling addict who occasionally featured as a poet but that is exactly what Charles Bukowski was: a wannabe writer who coped with constant rejection of his work by drowning himself in alcohol and slipping freefall into depression. He worked a menial job at the local post office and spent what meager income he earned doing more damage to himself- gambling and drinking himself to stupor on many occasions.

After thirty years of filtering away his life, a small-time editor discovered him and weirdly, offered him a contract. Bukowski accepted the contract even though it meant letting go of his single source of livelihood so far. That turned out to be his best decision so far. In less than a month, he had completed his first novel which, to everyone's consternation, fared successfully. He went on to be very successful and popular as a poet and novelist, selling millions of his books. Not only did Bukowski's rise stun the world, it stunned his very self.

So, as it turned out, you could say Bukowski was a poster boy for Never-Give-Up stories. He kept pushing and pushing and eventually hit his jackpot, so to speak. If anyone thought this, the inscription on his gravestone- "Don't Try"- argues otherwise. But why would such discouraging advice come from one who, by all appearances, won in the end? Maybe because he never saw himself as a winner. Bukowski's 'win' came from his unashamed acceptance of his status as a failed man. In fact, his writings were a brutally honest reflection of his undesirable life and somehow, that endeared him to his fans.

He was never one to be concerned about success; he was satisfied just being his horrible self. Even after attaining fame, he did not lose his drinking or his gambling. He still insulted his audiences publicly and did nothing to hide his perverted ways. He did not suddenly become a better version of himself because he became well-known, and it was definitely not because he transformed into the ideal human that he achieved his success. One common misconception in our world today is that becoming a better person is synonymous with becoming successful. The two concepts may go hand in hand often, but don't be deceived, they are not always the same thing.

We are so fixated on becoming our best selves, living our best lives, relating with the best people, etc. that we have lost track of reality. Motivational and self-help materials are not helping much because, unnoticed by many, they keep fixing our gazes on what we don't have and how we can go from where we are now to that picture-perfect happy place we all dream to be. They tell us how to date successfully, how to clinch a spouse, how to feel more beautiful, how to make more money and a whole lot of other How-To topics. Why? Because we don't see ourselves as being all those things yet. We're looking to improve ourselves. Think about it. If one were *really* happy, there'd be no need to read a book on how to be happy, would there?

Societal stereotypes and advertising messages want you to keep pushing; keep yearning for more. A better life, better kids, better partners, better jobs, you name it! Your insatiable concern for the next best thing in life only holds benefits for one thing, and it's not your health. It's business. The survival of commerce is dependent on your constant thirst for more. Your health, on the other hand, will be the worse for it. You don't need to have more to live a better life. Making so much fuss about too many things will only reduce the quality of your life. In fact, you should care about fewer things; stop expending your energy worrying about all those things you can do without. Concentrate on what is real, immediate and highly essential.

The human brain is such an interesting place, but it can also become sinister. If you're not careful, it can drive you nuts. Ever heard of the feedback loop? Here's how it works. Let's say for instance you find yourself getting angry very easily and at the slightest things. Then you get angry at the fact that you get angry all the time. It's made you such a horrible person and you're angry at yourself for what you've become. That's like triple-power anger and soon enough, it drives you totally over the edge. You do something unimaginable or destructive and you feel intense anger at yourself and maybe other people. Thus goes the destructive feedback loop. It's the same story with a myriad negative emotion- anxiety, worry, guilt, perfectionism, you name it.

Quite a number of people find themselves stuck in the feedback loop. Interestingly, the feedback loop is only possible because we have the ability to think about our thoughts, something other creatures cannot do. But the feedback loop is never a fun place to be. What's worse, today's acquisition-centered culture and the glamorous other world called social media continually feeds the loop by making us feel bad about having negative emotions. Back in the day, our grandparents and great-grandparents did not have filtered images of picture-perfect lives to compare theirs to. They also experienced negative emotions but it was easier for them to get over those emotions because they were not bombarded with so much evidence of everybody else appearing to be doing way better than they. For instance, you're having a bad day and decide to go on Facebook. Chances are that you'll end up feeling bad about the lousy day you're having because everyone else seems to be having the time of their lives; doing great things while you're just dragging your feet through life.

It's no surprise that this phenomenon has resulted in creating psychological wrecks; self-detesting, disturbed, and highly strung-out individuals going through life wondering what is wrong with them. You need to stop giving two cents about everything. You feel bad? So what? It's only natural to not feel good all the time. Don't give a hoot! By doing this, you'll be able to keep out of that dangerous loop.

The solution to all our anxiety issues and dissatisfaction with life stares us in the face but we have trouble seeing it. We enjoy benefits of living in a developed country yet anxiety, depression, and other related illnesses seem to have settled in our homes. We have so many opportunities that we only stay fixated on the next big thing; the 'More'. What many don't know is that our continuous desire for more or better signifies an undesirable experience while accepting our inadequacies signify a healthy state of being. The more you pursue adequacy, the more you'll feel inadequate.

You're probably wondering how you'll ever amount to something if you don't give a hoot about anything. But if you take time to notice- or you might already have- you'll see that it's those things you worry the least about that often turn out great. The negatives you try so hard to avoid are usually the ones that lead to the positives. Stop worrying so much about discomfort or things not going exactly as you want. Stop feeling so bad about it or you'll fall into a rut. Not giving a hoot means facing life's twists and turns head-on. It may sound so easy-peasy but there's a method to not giving a hoot about so many things.

We go through life fussing over every little thing; letting it get to us. Maybe if we remembered that death is inevitable, we'd realize how much we need to stop stressing. The trick here is to define what is totally important to you and what is not; to decide what is worth your attention only because it is absolutely necessary. It's not as easy as it sounds. Our default reaction is to stress over everything so this will take a lot of unlearning and re-engineering. It may even take you your entire life. But you'd rather do this than continue stressing over everything, letting the slightest discomfort get to you, and trapping yourself in a nasty feedback loop that will get you nowhere good.

Not giving a hoot, unlike what many assume, is not about becoming unaffected by anyone and anything. Far from it. So what does it really mean not to give a hoot? The following should help you understand better what all this is about:

- It means defining what is important to you and not giving a hoot when you come across challenges on your way. You know that challenges must come so you rise up to the challenge, not caring what anyone thinks about your methods. It's nothing to do with avoiding the discomfort in life, and everything to do with identifying which discomfort you'll bother your head about.

- Stressing over everything is a sign that you've got nothing significant to use your 'stress' on. If you're not going to give a hoot and stress over every little discomfort that comes your way, then you must have more significant stuff going on in your life, for which you can stress justifiably.
- Our default is to stress over everything! Notice how children seem to fuss and cry over the most insignificant things? As we grow, however, life experiences teach us how unnecessary so much of the things we bothered about are. Eventually, we get to a stage in life where our bodies are not as strong as they used to be; we do not have so much energy to waste anymore. So, we learn to prioritize and give a hoot about only those things 'hoot-worthy'. Consciously or unconsciously, we are constantly choosing what to stress over.

The premise of this book is that you take charge by identifying what is hoot-worthy and what is not. You need to come to an acceptance of the fact that challenges and discomfort are a part of life, even though they suck. You need to not feel bad about going through some uncomfortable times because it's only a part of life.

CHAPTER 2: HAPPINESS IS A PROBLEM

Key Takeaways:

- *Pain and disappointment are a necessary part of life*
- *Happiness comes from finding solutions to problems*
- *Problems are never-ending*
- *Emotions are basically evolved biological pointers*
- *Everyone has problems. Some just have better problems than others*

History tells us that the man called Buddha was born a crown prince, one whose father determined to shield from any form of suffering or discomfort. He was given everything in abundance and lacked nothing. Yet, he carried an emptiness that pushed him to run away from the idyllic home his father had built him. After seeing the real world and the intense suffering of people, the prince believed his life would become meaningful if he abandoned his riches and subject himself to suffering. After many years of suffering without any revelation of life mysteries as he'd hoped, the prince was forced to reconsider his idealistic view of suffering. After some reflection, he would come to understand that there was nothing so special about suffering. Everyone suffered- rich or poor, lavish or modest. Discomfort and loss are a part of life and trying to avoid them at all costs is a futile endeavor.

Most people erroneously believe that happiness is something to be earned systematically- do A and B and get happiness; Marry C to have a happy life; Buy so and so to be happy. Truth is, happiness exists alongside pain and disappointment that is an inextricable part of human life. Even natural science agrees with this. Evolutionary evidence shows us that dissatisfaction and discomfort are nature's mechanisms of spurring a man to better his lot. We are designed to keep looking for more than what we have.

Take for instance, hitting your toe on the table is sure to hurt. That's pain. But that pain serves a purpose. It is physical pain and it keeps us from doing those things that will hurt us physically; it keeps us within our limits. You're more likely to watch out for the table when next you're walking, aren't you? Or it makes you move the table out of the way. In both cases, the physical pain proved useful. Same goes for psychological pain.

When we go through experiences that hurt us emotionally, we become cautious to avoid the same experience or even anything similar. We become wary of making whatever mistakes we made that led to the pain. We become wiser. So when we try to avoid pain at all costs, we are also robbing ourselves of the benefits that come with it. We become cocooned in our idealistic creations and lose touch with reality.

Everyone experiences pain. Problems never cease. Some problems are just better than others. You solve one only to create a whole new set of others. Take for instance a man who decides to solve his health problem by signing up with a gym. Now he's going to deal with the problem of having to wake up in time as well as enduring the rigors of the session itself. A problem-free life is not possible. The most you can do is hope for the good problems.

Believe it or not, happiness is born in the course of solving these never-ending problems. In other words, ignoring your problems/discomfort and faking a perfect life is only sure to make you dejected. So basically, that fantasy of a problem-free life, ironically, only guarantees unhappiness. Happiness is not something that comes to you after ticking an item on your list. It is not something you can get from simply listening to certain teachings. It is created in the course of solving desirable problems, and because problems are never-ending, you can never reach the zenith of happiness. It's a work-in-progress.

Unfortunately, many folks refuse to accept this truth. They'd rather:

- Deny the presence of their problems, content to live in their own illusions; or
- Play the victim, believe that there's nothing they can do about their problems, and resign to a life of helplessness.

Both escape routes may be easier than actually solving the problem, but only in the short run. They provide that quick feeling of highness- much like alcohol does- but lead to insecurity, depression, despair, etc. Sadly, what most self-help experts prescribe is not much different from this.

Speaking words of affirmation while staring into the mirror may make you feel good short-term, but a lasting solution can be found only by solving the underlying problem. We all have ways of reducing the pain that comes with life's problems, but when we become totally reliant on these ways and continue to ignore our problems, we experience unimaginable pain when we eventually do face them.

As brutal as it may sound, emotions are basically evolved biological pointers meant to ensure our preservation. For instance, the pain felt when you touch a hot stove tells you not to do so again. Emotions exist to keep us away from the path that can wipe us out. It may sound quite shocking but that's the plain, biological truth. When you feel undesirable emotions, your brain is signaling for you to take an action- such as keeping away from a hot stove- and when you experience positive emotions, it's synonymous to a pat on the back for doing the right thing. But soon enough, the undesirable emotions will be back because, as mentioned earlier, problems are never-ending.

One must keep in mind however that emotions can be misleading, so the fact that you feel bad about something does not mean it is, and vice versa. There is danger in suppressing your emotions as well as in overindulging them. People who suppress their negative emotions lack the ability to solve their problems and consequently, are stuck in an unhappy rut. Those who overindulge their emotions, on the other hand, become addicted to the pursuit of something better; the pursuit of 'More'. They obsess over acquisitions and achievements as a means of remaining happy but it does nothing to satisfy their dissatisfaction. Whether we like it or not, our fantasies of a pain-free, problem-free, always-happy life can only be just that: a fantasy.

If someone were to ask you what you want from life, you'll probably have no problem answering. But what if you're asked the kind of pain you want in your life? Not so easy, right? But whether we like it or not, the latter is a more meaningful question than the former. Your answer to the first question is likely to be along the lines of happiness and sunny days but we must understand that we cannot have those without doses of pain and discomfort. Everyone wants the goodies but no one seems to be eager to pay the price.

Happiness is cloaked in pain. That unpleasant experience you're running from; within it lies your happiness. You must learn to own it and deal with it squarely, not ignore it. Embracing pain may not be the default for most of us, but if we're going to live happily in this problem-filled life, then we must start learning. Take a look at those who are seated at the top rung of the corporate ladder; they're usually those who embraced the pain and rigors of endless working hours and office politics.

CHAPTER 3: YOU ARE NOT SPECIAL

Key Takeaways:

- *Self-worth is not about how good a person feels about herself. It is about how she feels about her shortcomings*
- *Entitled people either feel they're too good or too bad*
- *We cannot all be extraordinary*
- *There's nothing wrong with regular*
- *Outstanding does not go hand-in-hand with a sense of entitlement*

Jimmy was one of those guys who always had something going on. He was always on to something. All you needed to do was ask how he was doing and you could get an earful of all the great stuff he had planned and all the big names he rolled with. Unfortunately, he was also a loafer who never seemed to actually kick off any of his much-publicized 'ideas'. He was content living off family and friends, and talking down anyone who was wise enough to point out his aimlessness. He would laugh at them for not recognizing the huge potential he carried. Jimmy's level of self-confidence was out of this world and no one could convince him how out-of-place it was. The few times he actually did make any money, it was usually through shady means.

The rave about high self-esteem did not become a thing until the 1960s. It became the 'in' thing in psychology after research revealed that folks with a high level of self-esteem were more likely to do great things and less likely to become public nuisances. So the craze to increase the number of people with high self-esteem was written into every aspect of our society- schools started to hand out underserved marks and trophies just to make kids feel better about themselves; motivational speakers began emphasizing how every one of us are capable of doing great things; clergymen told their congregation how incredibly special each one of them was.

Now, however, we see all that is wrong with that approach. We see that feeling good about oneself just for the fun of it is not helpful. We see that the experience of failure and hardship held back from that generation failed to turn out strong-willed individuals. Instead, there are a lot of Jimmy replicas, feeding fat on the sweat of others while feeling good about themselves, just for the fun of it.

Erroneously, the experts chalked up self-esteem as the good feelings folks had about themselves when it actually has more to do with how they feel about their undesirable characteristics. Like Jimmy, we now have a lot of folks who believe the sun rises and sets upon them. They believe they're absolutely wonderful, even when they're clearly making a mess of things. They believe they're special and should thus be treated. They feel entitled.

Such people have their heads up in the cloud, always. They strongly believe illusions of themselves which are often contrasting with reality. But who cares? They're confident in themselves and that's good, right? Self-confidence in itself is good; in fact, it can rub off on other people. But here's the catch: in keeping up with their illusions, entitled people do not mind who they hurt in the process. No matter how 'happy' these folks appear, they are not.

Want to know a person's self-esteem level? Go look at how he or she feels about and reacts to their shortcomings. Take a look at Jimmy. He refuses to acknowledge his inadequacies so he continues to make up stories of one castle in the air after another. He ignores his problems, acting as though they don't exist and he's the best thing to happen to the world. People with a high level of self-esteem do not deny their shortcomings. They own them and this makes it possible for them to work on said shortcomings.

Growing up was not exactly the smoothest ride: caught with marijuana at 13 and everything kinda went downhill from there. I was expelled from school and basically ostracized from my community. Then, my parents got divorced. I would spend the better part of my later years trying to free myself from the effects of these experiences. But that's not the point here. The point is that most of the trouble I experienced were as a result of everyone not saying things as they were. I'd say we were pretty good at evading.

When we experience traumatic stuff, there's the tendency to feel our problems are unique; things that no one has ever experienced; problems without solutions or to which the solution must be extremely special. We start feeling special ourselves, after all, we're experiencing 'special' problems.

This stage is just a step away from entitlement. That was what happened to me. I became entitled, and in a bid to convince myself that I was loved, went on an intimate relationship spree. My quest led me down a dangerous path as I began to hurt people's emotions without a care in the world. As long as I felt good with myself, I didn't care what the next person felt.

Entitled people usually fit into one of these two categories:

- Those who believe they should get special treatment because they're the best thing to happen to humanity
- Those who believe they should get special treatment because their lives are rap while every other person is fantastic.

The first category is usually easy to identify as a sense of entitlement. The second category is not always so obvious but still boils down to the same thing. Until you stop playing the ultimate victim and accepting that there's nothing unique or special about your problems, you won't be able to solve them and you can't be happy. Unfortunately, it appears more and more young people today are becoming entitled. The interconnectedness facilitated by the internet seems to have made us more selfish and insecure. We have the unrestrained freedom to stake our claims but have become increasingly intolerant of any other person's stand that does not support ours.

If we're being honest, we'll agree that the majority of human beings are quite regular in our day-to-day life. At most, we're probably extraordinary at one or two things and typical at the rest. There's absolutely nothing wrong with this. Our biological wiring does not support humans being exceptional at everything; there's just not enough energy for that! It's why you'll see outstanding businessmen and women finding it difficult to hold their personal relationships together. But no thanks to media- especially social media- the extraordinary is being portrayed as the norm. Regular does not make for popular media content so media agencies only publicize the best of the best. This reality passes across the message that we're inadequate. We want to be seen as better, so we resort to either of the two categories of entitlement.

More than ever before, people are having unrealistic expectations of themselves. The pervasiveness of media and marketing messages constantly pushes the agenda of a perfect, outstanding life and more people are feeling they do not measure up. The media are shaping people's perceptions of themselves and much of it is not positive. As much as the internet has been such a huge help in this generation, it has also opened the door for a myriad of self-esteem issues.

The self-esteem craze in the 1970s, combined with the effects of media and the internet, has succeeded in conditioning our minds to believe that we are all meant to be outstanding. The obvious error of this mindset is missed by most folks. If every one of us is outstanding, then there really would be none outstanding! But we don't see that, so we believe it's outstanding or nothing and detest any resemblance of average. We refuse to see any value for ourselves and others unless the 'outstanding' feature is visible. Anyone who is not outstanding does not mean much to us. This is why so many people have no sense of self-worth and do not value others as well.

The reality is, those who do achieve outstanding feats, do so not because they convinced themselves of how exceptional they are, but because they accepted their inadequacies and were able to work on them, getting better and better in the process. They did not start out entitled. Swallowing the mantra that we all are meant to be outstanding is much like eating junk food that will only harm your health.

But when you swallow life's bitter truths, when you accept that you may not be outstanding all your life and that it's okay to be regular, then you'll finally be in your good place. It is from this place that you can work towards your goals without carrying a pressing need to be exceptional. You would have released yourself from unrealistic expectations and be able to find joy in the basic pleasures of everyday life.

CHAPTER 4: THE VALUE OF SUFFERING

Key Takeaways

- *Suffering is non-negotiable; we can only choose what we suffer for*
- *Self-consciousness involves questioning the motive behind your feelings and actions*
- *Your values determine what you consider a success or failure*
- *There are good values and bad values; there are also bad success indicators and bad success indicators*
- *The quality of your values and success indicators determines the quality of your problems, and the quality of your problems determine the quality of your life*

The story is told of Hiroo Onoda, a Japanese soldier during the Second World War. At a time when the defeat of the Japanese side was imminent, Onoda was given orders to occupy Lubang, fight off the United States with everything in him, and never surrender. Within the next two months, the Americans had conquered Lubang. Onoda, with three of his men, hid successfully in the forest and from there carried out rebel attacks against the Americans and the local population. They couldn't do much, but every now and then, they would come out, attack as much as they could and run back into hiding.

Six months later, the war was declared over, with Japan conceding defeat. But Onoda and his men did not get the memo. Every now and then, they would still come out, attack civilians, steal food and supplies, and go back into hiding. They were making it difficult to rebuild the war-ravaged cities and the governments- Japan and USA decided to do something about it. They distributed flyers pronouncing that the war was over and urging every soldier to go back home. Onoda and his men saw these but refused to heed.

Twenty-five years later, and after many more batches of flyers being distributed, these men were still in hiding and constantly wreaking havoc on nearby civilian communities. These communities eventually started to fight back and succeeded in killing Onoda's men, leaving him all alone in the jungle. The Japanese government conducted various searches that turned out fruitless. Onoda became a sort of mythical figure whom many assumed dead.

But this would soon change when an adventurous young man, Norio Suzuki, decided to take on the search for Onoda as his next big thrill. Totally unprepared, he ventured into the jungle. His 'strategy' was laughable, especially considering the fact that highly trained search teams had been deployed earlier for the same task without any success. By simply roaming the jungle, yelling Onoda's name, and telling him how worried the Emperor was about him, Suzuki was able to do- in just four days- what the search teams failed at.

Suzuki and Onoda hit it off and both men found out they were more alike than they knew. While Onoda had refused to vacate the jungle simply because he was ordered- almost thirty years ago- to never surrender, Suzuki was a young, adventurous young man who chased thrill after thrill regardless of how unrealistic they were. Not too long after his meeting with Onoda, Suzuki would die on yet another of his adventures. These men both dedicated their lives to pursuits that were in no way comfortable. In fact, they were downright risky and life-threatening.

Their lives are a perfect description of what obtains in reality. We all have to face problems or suffer; that's non-negotiable. The question is what we choose to suffer for. They both chose their paths of suffering and even though it might seem absurd to many, those cause must have meant something to them. Otherwise, why would a man spend the greater part of his years hiding in a jungle and risking his life countless times or the other go off on dangerous escapades that would eventually cost him his life? It's simple: They both wanted their chosen suffering so they found it easier to tolerate.

Self-consciousness can be likened to an onion. The more you peel back its unending tiers, the more you're likely to be driven to tears. The first tier has to do with being able to recognize our emotions. For many of us, we fall short even in this seemingly simple task. You would think it'd be easy to know when you're happy or when you're sad but for most people, emotional blind spots are a reality. We might have been raised to find the expression of certain emotions unacceptable and we go through life hiding or denying the same emotions.

The second tier addresses the reason or motive behind our emotions. In many cases, this inquiry requires the assistance of a therapist who tries to unravel the foundation of what we deem fit to be called success or failure.

A third tier, which is often more gut-wrenching, has to do with why something amounts to success with us and why another amounts to failure. It has to do with our core ideals and tenets as individuals. It's not always easy unraveling this level but when we do, it makes all the difference because when we identify our principles, we can identify what constitutes problems to us, we get to realize the things we care about and ultimately establish the quality of our lives.

Most people would rather ignore this third level because it can be very complex and revealing. They'd rather keep denying their problems or heaping the blame on others while playing the victim. Many counseling professionals also pay no heed to this tier because it's easier to address what a person claim is wrong with him or her than delve into the why of the problem. For instance, a person comes and says how unhappy he is because he doesn't have money and they go on to give tips on how he'll make more money. But they refuse to address why the need to make money is so important and valuable to him in the first place.

What conventional approach does is make people happy for a while; give folks tips they can fall back on when that initial burst of happiness fades. So, they become addicted to these tips and the situation is no different from that of a cocaine user snorting occasionally to get his high. Probing oneself sincerely is not always the easiest or most comfortable thing to do, but it helps to reveal the real motives behind your feelings, emotions, and actions. If you give a hoot so much about something, it's very likely that you associate that with some form of shortcoming or inadequacy on your part. If you can get to this stage, you can honestly ask yourself if that shortcoming is really as you see it or if you've been looking at it wrongly the whole time.

The story of legendary guitarist, Dave Mustaine reveals a lot about human nature. Rejected and humiliated by his former band, Mustaine determined to succeed at all costs. His desire for revenge fueled his ambition and he succeeded in creating a new band which became highly popular and sold more than 25 million albums worldwide. To many, Mustaine and his band, Megadeth was highly successful. The only problem was that Mustaine had set his standard for success as outdoing his former band, Metallica, and since they went on to sell over 180 million album copies worldwide, Mustaine still felt like he had failed. Because his success indicator was set in comparison to Metallica, Mustaine was unable to recognize the incredible feats he achieved and all the popularity and acceptance his band had.

This behavior, evident in many of us, makes us no different from our evolutionary brothers, the apes. We keep measuring ourselves against others and end up feeling good

ONLY when we outdo those and establish our status as better than the others. We may think Mustaine was quite unreasonable but the same goes for every one of us. Our success indicators or standard may differ from his, but at the end of the day, these indicators determine what we consider as success or failure. And those indicators are informed by our individual values. These ultimately determine how we perceive our problems. The story of Pete Best depicts this accurately.

He was the drummer who started out with the globally acclaimed Beatles. He was kicked out just at the threshold of their massive popularity and in no time, his life seemed to take a downward turn. At the end of the day however, he was quoted as saying he had a happier life than he would have had had he stayed on with the group. Now Best did not achieve as much as Mustaine did, but why did he have such a positive conclusion when Mustaine's was negative. Simple. Best had a whole new set of values. He narrated how his firing from the group led to him meeting his wife and having a wonderful family. He began to see a happy family life as of more value than the fame and riches of being with a popular band. So, while Mustaine sold millions of albums worldwide and thought of himself as a failure, Best did not sell as much and still considered himself successful.

This goes to prove that there are positive values and negative values, just as there are positive success indicators and vice versa. The quality of your values and success indicators determines the quality of your problems. The following are some ideals to which we subscribe, that we should do without:

Gratification- everyone wants to feel good, but when it becomes a principle with which you drive your actions, you're likely to end up in trouble. Unfortunately, in today's world of mass marketing, this is what is constantly pushed before our faces as ideal. It is what propels a drug addict to keep taking the next snort until there is no more life left with which to take a snort, or what keeps a spouse cheating until the home is shattered.

Material wealth- prioritizing material possessions and acquisitions leads to an increase in shallow, superficial individuals, and the world definitely needs less of that.

Being right always- no one learns by claiming to know it all. Folks who feel good about themselves only when they're right find it hard to function as part of a society. They lack the ability to entertain other people's perspectives with an open mind. Ultimately, they find it difficult to achieve real growth.

Ignoring negative emotions- so many people prioritize the need to keep a sunny disposition about everything, no matter how distressing it is. Sadly, remaining positive all the time only means you're denying negative emotions and refusing them expression does not automatically make them disappear. It's okay, helpful even, to accept the fact that bad things are bad things. Life is not always great and it's okay to feel bad about it. Forcing yourself to remain upbeat about everything equals denying your problems.

You can't solve problems you don't acknowledge and you deny yourself the happiness we get from solving problems.

Excellent principles, such as non-violence, honesty, and humility are realistic, beneficial to others (even though it may not guarantee instant gratification), and can be controlled by you. Undesirable values, such as violence and instant gratification usually have to do with events outside of yourself. Your individual principles all boil down to one thing: Choice. What do you place more premium on? From the examples of Best and Mustaine, we see a difference in values upheld by each man. Those values influenced their decisions and defined their understanding of success and failure respectively.

As such, choosing the wrong values leads us to giving a hoot about so many things we shouldn't, as in Mustaine's case. The key to making yourself better is choosing better values because then you can bother yourself with the things you should, get to deal with better quality of problems, and ultimately have a better life.

CHAPTER 5: YOU ARE ALWAYS CHOOSING

Key Takeaways:

- *Problems you willingly choose give you a sense of empowerment while those imposed on you elicit a feeling of oppression*
- *Responsibility is not synonymous with fault*
- *Someone else might be at fault for your situation, but only you are responsible*
- *True growth cannot occur until you take responsibility*
- *Lose the feeling of entitlement; it's not cool to play 'victim'.*

There exists a significant difference between a problem of your own making and one that you're coerced into. Take for instance, being asked to run a certain number of miles and failure to do so will bring harm to your loved ones. In another scenario, you run the same number of miles in a marathon you thoroughly trained for. There will always be problems, but what makes one tolerable and another painful is a function of how you came to be in that problem: did you willingly choose it or were you coerced into it?

William James, the renowned father of American Psychology, had a very rough start in life. He was born of wealthy parents but right from birth, suffered debilitating ailments- volatile stomach, partial blindness, hearing problems, and back tremors that made sitting or standing upright impossible. He wasn't the brightest kid and next to his brilliant siblings, he was considered a weird kid. He failed at painting. He failed at Medicine. He failed at expedition. His own father saw him as a disgrace to the family.

Finally, almost thirty and at the end of his tether, James decided he wasn't of much use alive. Before killing himself, he stumbled upon an idea for an experiment. He had been reading the works of a philosopher, Charles Pierce, and he resolved to give himself one more year during which he would believe that he was completely responsible for everything that happened in his life. His belief would propel him to do everything possible to improve his situation, but if he failed to make any changes, he would accept his helplessness and do away with his own life. That experiment was his turning point. James would go on to become highly respected in the academic community and have a family of his own.

No real progress or development can be achieved until we take responsibility for everything in our lives. We may have no power over what happens to us, but how we choose to see and react to those things, is totally on us. Consciously or unconsciously, we carry the responsibility for our encounters. It's just default. Even if we choose not to react to certain events, our choice in itself is a reaction to the event.

Every day, in every situation, we are selecting our values and standards and making judgments informed by them. Sometimes it's conscious; other times, we don't even know we're doing it. We can*not* care about something. Our focus should be on what we care about; what we deem attention-worthy. Are the values and standards that inform our judgments and actions good or bad?

We've all heard the quote "with great power comes great responsibility" but we may not know that it's more profound the other way round. Yes, with great responsibility comes great power. The more you accept responsibility for your experiences, the more power you'll wield over your life. Remember, you can't solve your problems without accepting responsibility for them.

The popular misconception is that responsibility equals fault. It is possible to be responsible for what is going on in your life without it being your fault. Take for instance a judge assigned a case. The judge did not commit the crime neither did the judge choose to be on that case. It's not the judge's fault but it is now her responsibility. While fault is as a result of something you've done in the past, responsibility is more real-time. It concerns the choices you're making on how to respond to what has already been done.

You see, a lot of people may be at fault for your situation, but nobody else but you is responsible. It is you who decides (whether you're aware of it or not) how to react in any situation. It is you who decides what standards to uphold at any given time and what to give a hoot about. Until you accept that responsibility, you will continue to whine about how unfair life is and how everyone else but you has it good.

When my girlfriend cheated on me with her teacher, I was devastated. We'd been together for three years but she did not show the slightest bit of hesitation to leave me for him. I was hurt and bitter and laid the responsibility for my unhappiness at her feet. I soon realized however that although she was at fault for making me feel the way I did, she was not responsible. I was. It was up to me to get myself out of the rut. It was better from then on out. I had accepted responsibility for my unhappiness and that enabled me to take steps towards solving my problem; restoring my happiness.

Taking responsibility also does something wonderful to you as a person. In my case, I soon began to look back and see areas where I had fallen short in the relationship. It didn't absolve my girlfriend of the horrible thing she did but it made me realize that I also contributed to my unhappiness. I wasn't a saint. I was also able to reflect on all the things that had been going wrong for so long but which I was content to ignore. My discoveries helped me to know what mistakes not to repeat so as not to experience the same pain a second time. I was able to become a better me. As it turned out, the same experience that causes me untold pain and misery became the one that inspired so much of my personal improvement. Until we take responsibility for our lives, we will not grow.

Owning up to responsibility in a relationship break-up can however not be compared to doing the same in a catastrophic situation. When weightier matters are in play, especially when it concerns serious injury or loss of life, accepting responsibility is a whole different ballgame. But whether we like it or not, the principle of assuming responsibility stays the same. No matter how tragic a situation is, you still have to take responsibility for how you react and what you do about the situation. Take the case of Malala Yousafzai for instance. At just age fourteen, she was shot in the head in a move to silence her activism. She miraculously survived and although the shooting wasn't her fault, she took responsibility and responded by intensifying her efforts, for which she would receive a Nobel Peace Prize award for in 2014. She could have resigned to silence but she chose to respond otherwise. Either way, whatever choice she made would have been a function of her exercising her responsibility to react in a certain way.

BBC, in 2013, did a feature on six teenagers who were suffering from Obsessive Compulsive Disorder, more commonly known as OCD. The idea was to document their therapy efforts at overcoming the condition. Interestingly, managing OCD comes right back to the issue of choosing better principles and success indicators. One of the very first steps to managing the condition is to tell people with OCD to accept the inadequacies of their obsessive wishes. They need to accept that life is not perfect. Bad things will happen and it's not as a result of them not obeying their compulsions.

Next, they are urged to adopt better values other than those that have informed their compulsive desires for so long. Adopting and internalizing these values is what shapes new actions, different from what their obsessive nature would dictate. The process is not always easy. It comes with a lot of highs and lows, but with consistency, a change can be achieved. They are better able to manage their obsessive traits. People with OCD- or any other birth defects for that matter- are not to blame for their conditions, but they are responsible for how they respond to it.

We can learn a lot from poker. A player might be dealt good cards and still lose to another player with lousy cards. The one with good cards has higher chances of winning but at the end of the day, it boils down to what kind of decisions each player makes while playing. We may have no choice in certain situations we find ourselves but we can decide to make the best of it. We can decide how we want to respond. Be it neurological defects, physical and sexual abuse, or loss of a dear one, we all get one or more of those things that seem to be imposed on us unfairly, but that doesn't excuse the fact that we still have a responsibility to choose how to respond to these things.

The misconception of fault versus responsibility has seen many folks avoiding to take responsibility for their lives. They take the person or thing at fault and bestow such with a responsibility and power that should really be theirs. They max out their victim card and enjoy the false saintly feeling that comes with it. Unfortunately in modern times, the internet and social media has made it an effortless endeavor.

These days, everyone is playing the victim and it gets worse because your claims of victimization can be broadcast to a global audience, generating interest and validation for your outbursts. The slightest hint of offense is emphasized and blasted across the World Wide Web where an army of audiences exists to share and rebroadcast said claims. We are becoming highly intolerant, entitled individuals who feels their oppression is superior and demands more attention than any other's. Sadly, this trend has also created an atmosphere where it is difficult to identify people who are actually victims. We forget that the democracy we clamor for requires us to acknowledge other views and perspectives because we all have free expression.

If you're wondering how to go about changing your values and taking responsibility for your life, then you're walking the wrong path. This is pretty simple. It's either you do it or you don't. If you're asking how to go about it, then you're unconsciously making a choice that is not aligned with taking responsibility. Surely, it's no easy ride but the results are absolutely worth it. You'll face obstacles almost every step of the way. You'll wonder if you really are doing the right thing or if you can really handle giving up those undesirable ideals. You'll face situations and take decisions that will make you feel like you're failing. Your standard for success and failure is changing so it's expected that you'll get confused somewhere along the line. It's also likely that you'll lose some relationships; alliances that will become uncomfortable with your new way of life. This is expected. It will hurt. You'll feel a lot of pain. Heck! You'll constantly feel that you're mistaken. But in the long run, you'll begin to give a hoot about the things that really matter and the quality of your life will improve.

CHAPTER 6: YOU'RE WRONG ABOUT EVERYTHING (BUT SO AM I)

Key Takeaways:

- *Wrong is good; Right is not*
- *Your brain is not reliable*
- *Accepting your wrongness is a basis for learning and growth*
- *Don't know yourself*

We've all been wrong before. If we're being honest we've all been wrong at every point in our lives before. Women once thought applying dog urine on their faces slowed down aging. California was once thought to be an island. Yes, we've all been wrong before but the problem is with how we perceive it. Being wrong is good. When you look back and realize all those things you were wrong about, it means you've learned. The 'You' of today can identify the errors of the 'You' in the past. So also, the 'You' in future should look back at the present 'You' and identify mistakes.

Real learning and growth only take place when you're constantly wrong about everything. Almost all of us will agree that growth never stops, but then we're so obsessed with finding the accurate answer to everything. That's not how it works, because if we already find the absolute right answer, what need is there to keep learning and growing?

We should only be interested in becoming less wrong than we were the previous day. There's no shame in having a different answer from the one you gave yesterday because you're only human. You change.

Obsession with being right about our lives can prevent us from living it and taking chances for growth. We hold on to a particular 'truth' about ourselves and refuse to challenge it. We'd rather stay safe than face uncertainties to improve ourselves. It is no wonder then that one of the pre-requisites for growth is an acceptance of your values' uncertainties and imperfections.

Don't look to be sure all the time. Look out for how uncertain you are. Accepting that you're wrong all the time makes you receptive to change and improvement.

The human brain is a funny place. What we hold as beliefs and convictions today are as a result of our brains making associations between more than several experiences. But here's the catch: our brains are not perfect. You have no idea how easy it is for the brain to register a misconception on our part as truth. This is why you may go into a situation and misinterpret it, yet your brain registers it as truth and you continue to believe your own misconception. But that's not all. Our brain also keeps constant with the interpretation we feed it.

Consequently, most of what we have come to believe today are end products of inherent prejudice and misconception. Many of the principles that guide our lives today are products of a faulty process that involves individual experiences. This is not exactly comforting news, but it is essential that we accept it if we intend to grow.

The Meredith Maran case is very significant. In 1980, the 37-year old journalist accused her biological father of sexually abusing her when she was little. She had forgotten the incident and only just remembered as an adult during her therapy session. Expectedly, her accusation tore the family apart. Eight years later however, Maran would realize that she had somehow conjured the event. It never actually happened. The damage was done though. Her father never reconciled with her and her family was left in shambles. Interestingly, the 1980s saw a lot of cases like Maran's: women accusing male relatives of sexual abuse only to retract their stories years later.

The phenomenon can be attributed to our memory's modus operandi. Usually, when we experience something, our memory does not replay it exactly as it was. In trying to relay it to someone else, we fill in the gaps left by our memory with conjured details of our own. Then we find ourselves constantly inventing new stuff, adding and removing from the event, until one day it is half-lies. In most cases, we don't mean any harm, but in others- like Maran's- we end up causing a lot of problems for a lot of people, not to mention ourselves. The workings of the brain is such that it carries out its functions, but not perfectly. It is not fool-proof.

One of the reasons for this is that the brain is designed to make new inferences based on the information we have stored already. So when you're on good terms with an individual, your brain is likely to interpret any action from such individual positively. The reverse is the case when you associate an individual with negative feelings such as hatred or suspicion.

Now enter Maran, a feminist who did not have the best of relationships with her father. She had also done a lot of child abuse research which brought her in close contact with survivors of incestuous relationships. She seemed to have no luck with relationships herself, having a failed marriage along with a string of failed relationships. She was in a toxic relationship with a female incest survivor. Her homosexual orientation did not help her tumultuous relationship with her father. So, when her therapist pushed her to dig into her past for traumatic experiences, it wasn't difficult for her brain to associate all these experiences and provide an aligning 'result'.

Our brain is unreliable, and so is our memory. It is not enough to trust your instincts. It is dangerous, considering the fact that your instincts are largely biased. The key is to keep probing our beliefs. Again, this may not immediately sound like the best advice you've ever got but in it lies the potential for growth.

When psychologist, Roy Baumeister embarked on a quest to understand why people do bad things, he did not imagine he'd find that most of them felt so good about themselves. Contrary to the existing theory that low self-worth was what made people do evil, an unflinching certainty in one's rightness is actually one of the hallmarks of mean people. They believe they are right, irrespective of what anyone around them says; irrespective of what the reality is. A suicide bomber will murder millions simply because he believes in his right standing and moral uprightness. Irrespective of whatever he sees to the contrary, he believes he is doing the right thing and will be rewarded in heaven.

Folks who refuse to accept the impossibility of certainty end up exhibiting insecurity. They find themselves in a perpetual state of dissatisfaction that leads to them feeling slighted. They start believing they are at a disadvantage and deserve to be attended to; entitlement all over again. Embracing doubt, on the other hand, brings everything good. Asides from the ultimate benefit of enabling you learn and grow, doubt implies that you're wrong about everything. So you learn to stop making unwarranted assumptions about other people and yourself. You lose the default bias that controlled you for so long. You become more open to trying out new things.

Your present set of principles, no matter how convenient, should not be cast in stone. You must accept that you're wrong about everything so you can keep exploring everything. You must first acknowledge and accept your wrongness before taking any steps towards solving your problem. You must accept that you've been doing it wrong all this while; that you've been feeding fat on your own smug ignorance.

The crux of Manson's Law of Avoidance is that we humans avoid anything that has potential to disturb our present view of ourselves. We'd rather stay in our comfort zone, knowing for sure where we belong in the world, than try new things and new experiences. You're sure of your role as a decent wife so you'd rather endure a crappy sex life than tell your husband about it. You don't want to threaten your image as a tolerant friend so you avoid telling your friend you're no more interested in the friendship.

For so long, you have steered your life according to certain principles. You're partial towards them and your brain has picked up the signal, reinforcing them. You'd do anything to stay within your comfort zone; your certainty zone. But real change cannot come until you discard preset beliefs about yourself. Unlearn everything you've learned and remain in a perpetual state of doubt. Stop believing you know yourself and be open to not knowing. Only then can you continue learning and growing.

Doing away with all the conceptions you've built about yourself frees you to explore; get things done without the pressure of trying to live up to an identity. When you remain fixated on the certainties in your life, you're indirectly saying how one-of-a-kind you are, and that's only one step away from feeling entitled. Discard all those things you've told yourself about the uniqueness of your problems; how no one else is you because you're YOU. You're probably wondering if this is the right thing to do. No doubt, it's not easy to go from feeling special and unique to telling yourself you're just like everybody else, but in the long run, it makes you a better person.

Asking yourself these questions will help as you work some doubt into your life:

- What if I've got it wrong?
- What implications does my being wrong have?
- Would being wrong create better or worse problems for me and other people?

CHAPTER 7: FAILURE IS THE WAY FORWARD

Key Takeaways:

- *Failure and Success are inseparable*
- *Failure teaches profound lessons*
- *Failure is necessary for growth and improvement*
- *Pain can be good for you*
- *The trick is to just do something!*

Hardly would anyone call being jobless, penniless, and homeless, a good thing. For me, however, this post-college situation was beneficial. Why? Because I found myself at the lowest rungs of life and the only other place to go was up. I didn't have to carry the fear of failing anymore because fresh out of college, I was already a failure in many ramifications.

One of the most interesting thing about failure is that it is relative. My definition of failure might be different from the next person's, depending on what standards we measure it by. From a young age, I had known that a lack of money did not amount to failure. Grew up in a family that had no money worries, but I also got to see first-hand how inconsequential money was when it came to happiness.

I placed premium rather on independence. So when I had to choose between waiting for a response to any of my many resumes and starting up my own internet business, it was an easy pick.

There is a paradoxical relationship between failure and success. A certain woman once offered to buy Pablo Picasso's napkin doodle. When she heard his price, she was astonished and told him he had done the drawing in a short time. He replied by telling her it had actually taken him sixty years. Making progress is usually a function of how many times you've fallen. See anyone very good at what they do? Then they've had lots of failures at that same thing. You cannot achieve legitimate, lasting success without rubbing shoulders with failure.

A toddler learning to walk eventually succeeds only after many fails. You don't see her giving up after the first fail, do you? Unfortunately, somewhere along the line, we all pick up the societal signal that failure is to be detested. Our performance-based education system and media portrayal of perfection are some of the agents to blame for this misconception. As a result, we avoid failure. We avoid anything that may lead to failure. We avoid anything unfamiliar and stick with the comfortable. We forfeit any chance of growth and success.

Once again, we can trace this problem to choosing bad values. When our definition of success is tied to the actions of others, we're bound to always fall short and declare ourselves failures. Not only do these values leave us feeling anxious a lot of the time, they also leave us feeling worthless once the standard has been attained. For instance, defining success by the purchase of a house only keeps you happy until you buy that house. Problem solved;

Unhappiness sets in. This is why setting goals only provide satisfaction as long as they're yet to be achieved.

When Kazimierz Dabrowski commenced his research on how World War Two survivors dealt with the suffering and pain that came with the war, he did not expect them to show gratitude for the war. No, they weren't happy that there was a war, but they did reveal that experiencing the horrors of war made them better persons in the long run. They had a new-found appreciation for their loved ones and life itself. They became less shallow. They bothered less about life's frivolities. They gave a hoot only over the most necessary things.

Their experience is not different from what obtains with every other human. Some of our most painful encounters have birthed in us significant growth and improvement. Pain is a non-negotiable part of life, and is not always to be avoided. Be it physical or emotional pain, we need the jolts to become better, stronger versions of ourselves, physically and emotionally.

For so many of us, we have been held back from doing the things we want to do because of the fear of pain. We would gladly try so many new things if only the attendant pain is taken out of the equation. But this fear only holds us back from facing our problems and taking the first step to solving them. If you're making the choice to turn in your messed up values for the good ones, anticipate pain. Embrace it and live it out. The answer is not to ignore the pain or make it go away by falling to your old habits. Pain works a change in you that no pleasure on earth can.

Earlier on, I knew I wanted to start my own business, but I had no idea what that really entailed until I quit my day job. I suddenly realized the enormity of what I was about to embark on and promptly freaked out. I was exhausting my account and knew I had to do something fast. Even though I wasn't still sure what I was doing, I just did something. It taught me a great lesson: that doing something, in itself, is a potent source of drive and inspiration.

Many of us are waiting to feel inspired before we do anything, but it doesn't always work that way. Doing something can serve as the motivation you need to get your plans in motion. This will help shift your perspective on what constitutes success or failure. Adopting this approach also makes it easier for you to adopt new values that are beneficial to your life. Shifting lanes is never easy. Moving from the familiar to the unfamiliar comes with a significant amount of discomfort, and if you overthink it, you might end up trying to avoid the pain by resorting to your old ways. The trick is to just do something!

CHAPTER 8: THE IMPORTANCE OF SAYING NO

Key Takeaways:

- *Rejection is required for a balanced, meaningful life*
- *You cannot fully enjoy the experience of something or someone unless you commit*
- *Healthy love does not entail taking responsibility for your partner's actions or passing responsibility of your actions to your partner.*
- *Learn to give and take rejection; Learn to say and hear "NO"*
- *Trust is created only when partners are comfortable with telling each other the truth, no matter how bitter*
- *There is significance and fulfillment in being dedicated to one thing; Less is More*

At age 25, my internet business was fetching me a decent sum. I packed up my bags one day and left to travel the world, meet new people, create new experiences. Those were my handy reasons however. There was more to my 'brave' move. I was a man trying to make up for his lost teenage years and I did this to an excess. I was traveling the world because hey, I wasn't that socially-awkward teenager anymore. I could talk to anybody, hook up with anybody, and do anything I wanted with anybody. I was free, and who's to stop me from enjoying my freedom to the full?

So I went, and I spoke to many people, and made many friends, and had sex with lots of women. You could say I was living the life, yet it had no significance; no meaning. My current quiet life is more fulfilling than my days of exploring and enjoying my freedom. Here's what I took from that experience: absolute freedom is only a means to an end, and not an end in itself. The key to attaining that height of significance is to refuse absolute freedom; to remain steadfast. Only when you invest yourself in a single entity do you experience the sense of meaning that comes with it.

Russian culture teaches a profound lesson. There is a certain frankness to their interactions, which I initially chalked up as rudeness. There were no polite smiles or pretentious conversations. There were no undeserved remarks to be handed out. They said things just as it is and didn't seem to care much for what the other person thinks. Coming from the West, and having grown up in a home where we excelled at bottling everything up, this was strange for me. Soon enough however, I got used to it and came to realize the power in being blunt. I began to question the quality of interactions where I came from. It was so different from the Russians' yet it appeared to be working for the Russians.

A note-worthy explanation is that Russians, in coping with communism, have had to value and depend on the quality of trust. As such, it was required of everyone to be candid, even if it meant being brutally honest. It was a matter of survival. The West on the other hand, has its free marketplace that allowed all and sundry to participate.

Competition soon necessitated the need to keep up better appearances than the next man; the need to express the opposite of what you really feel; the need to lie just to convince someone to buy; buying something not because you need it but because it makes you look good. We have become very good liars. The result: trust has become a scarce commodity.

This same consumerist culture tells us to be agreeing of everything. Don't say no. Explore everything. Unfortunately, this only leaves us aimless because when you stand for everything, you end up standing for nothing. We need to embrace rejection as a part of life. To get the most of anything or even anyone, commitment is necessary. Consequently, commitment to one thing means rejection of other substitutes.

The very act of choosing certain principles dictates a denunciation of others. If you're all about directing your life in line with good values, you'd be unwise to still hold on to bad values. Avoiding rejection makes it impossible for you to know where you stand, so you drift, faceless. Rejecting things or people will be hard, especially when those things or people are the familiar part of your world. But if you're determined to adopt better values, you will have to swallow the bitter pill. Trying to avoid rejection is also another twisted form of entitlement. You don't want to feel bad for offending anyone and anything when you say "No", so you say "Yes" to everything and end up in confusion.

So just as you're learning to get comfortable saying "No", learn to get comfortable hearing it as well.

Shakespeare's "Romeo and Juliet" is closer to a depiction of love in modern times than in Shakespeare's time. Two lovers taking rash and irrational decisions. They're more 'crazy' than 'in love' and eventually take their lives as a result of their love. Sadly, these days we're obsessed with the crazy, irrational, roller-coaster aspects of romantic love. Love- the right kind- is not about public displays of affection or outbursts of emotion. The right kind of love involves two people who accept responsibility for their individual lives and are not afraid to give or take rejection if the need arises. The reverse is what a toxic relationship looks like.

Entitlement once again makes an appearance in this concept of love. Whether in a romantic or family relationship, or even in friendships, entitled people always find a way not to take responsibility for their problems. Healthy relationships have partners who each accept responsibility for their own actions, while providing support for each other. In their case, giving support is a choice and has nothing to do with one party being entitled.

Interestingly, entitled people- the ones who push the responsibility of their actions to others and the ones who take on responsibility for the actions of others- are usually drawn to each other. Eventually however, they are unable to satisfy each other and only end up making each other worse. If the love was the real and healthy kind, the victim would stop pushing responsibility to the partner, and the saver would stop taking on the responsibility of the partner.

There's usually a thin line between doing something out of entitlement and doing it because you want to. So when you're not sure, ask yourself what would happen if you did not take responsibility or what would happen if your partner did not do something you want her to do. If you're honest, and your answer involves something similar to a fight breaking out, then that's a red flag right there. Real love is not giving a hoot over everything your partner gives a hoot about. It's giving a hoot about your partner!

Any relationship where partners place a premium on making each other feel good is bound to hit the rocks sooner or later. I'm not saying become a horrible monster to your partner, but if you have to lie just because you don't want the other to feel bad, then something is fundamentally wrong. I tell my wife the truth when she asks me how she looks. On the few occasions when she looks awful and I tell her, she gets offended but in the long run, she loves me for it because I save her from looking awful in front of many people. Same goes for me. My wife is always honest with me, and sometimes that honesty hurts, my ego fees slighted, but at the end of the day, I wouldn't have it any other way because it is what makes us better people.

You do not always have to agree. In fact, you should not. If you're scared to say "No" to each other, then your relationship is toxic and trust cannot be forged. Trust is created when both parties are sure to get the truth- no matter how bitter- from each other. And trust is non-negotiable in a mutually beneficial relationship. When someone cheats, the grave offense is not really the act of having sex with another. It's the trust that has been broken.

Cheating is usually a function of one partner prioritizing something else above their relationship, like pleasure or the validation that comes from sex. So when a cheating partner says he or she won't do it again, it's not that simple. Until they take the time to reassess their values and strip their self-awareness onion; until they identify and acknowledge those messed up values that got them cheating in the first place; until they bid those values goodbye and prioritize the relationship, they won't get to address the real issue and trust cannot be restored.

Actions also speak louder than words, so until a cheating person consistently proves by their actions that they can now be trusted, the situation still remains the same. And this goes for any relationship- friendship, family- where trust has been broken. Until the guilty party identifies and acknowledges the faulty values, and until they prove, with their actions, that they can now be trusted, it's still a broken trust situation.

For a long time, we have been conditioned to believe that 'more is more'- more sexual partners, more cash, more opportunities. But the plain truth is that when we have too many choices, we often find it difficult to make any particular choice, so we fuss over all and end up dissatisfied. We're scared of picking one and losing all the other 'great' choices so we don't make a choice at all. We have it all. But the problem with that is it robs us of having a significant experience with anything and leaves us feeling like we missed something.

On the other hand, when you remain dedicated to one thing- one partner, one career, one endeavor- you're more likely to find the experience highly rewarding and fulfilling. You experience the substance of depth instead of the frivolity of breadth; quality over quantity. When you say "No" to all the many experiences and principles you've been chasing for so long, and commit to a few that are of high premium, you'll come to realize how much more unrestricted you'll be. Yes, there's a liberty that comes with focusing only on the things that matter; not giving a hoot about every damn thing; being okay with saying "No".

CHAPTER 9: . . . AND THEN YOU DIE

Key Takeaways:

- *Accepting the reality and inevitability of death gives you power to make your life count*
- *Your insane activity and the fact that you care about too many things are fueled by an innate fear of death*

It would take the death of my childhood friend to jolt me from the non-existence I confined myself to. After Josh died, I became depressed and miserable. He had been someone I looked up to. We would talk about our plans for the future and all the awesomeness we would bring to the world. But all that came to an end when influenced by alcohol, Josh jumped off a cliff at a party he invited me to.

For the longest time, I wondered what the point of life was. Then one day, after seeing Josh in a dream, I got the most revolutionary insight of my life. I realized that if there was no point to life, if death was something that would come sooner or later, then I had no reason to let my fears overwhelm me. I should go out there and do stuff; get out of my comfort zone that was keeping me bound; throw away those messed up values that I'd been so scared of letting go; become a better me!

What followed this realization is till today, the biggest turnaround of my life. I cleaned up my act, got rid of the familiar rubbish I had accustomed myself to, and determined to be the best I could. In a weird twist, it too Josh dying to get me to really live. We don't like to think about death, even when it's staring us in the face. But it is a part of life, and in a strange sort of way, accepting the reality and inevitability of death is what enables us to make our lives truly meaningful.

Despite having a doctorate in anthropology, Ernest Becker was a pariah in the academic community. Not only was he never on good terms with his superiors, he also subscribed to the weirdest ideas and teaching methods. Not surprisingly, he was always out of a job. After moving around four jobs in the space of six years, he was diagnosed with cancer. And it was on his deathbed that Becker would author a book that, years later, still impacts the world with its profound submissions. The book, written about death, notes that:

- Human beings have the unique ability to reflect about themselves. We can see ourselves in imaginary situations and make projections. One of those situations is death. You and I can think about the unavoidable occurrence of death and that thought creates in us a very real fear of death.
- Every human being consists of the physical self and the conceptual self. Our physical, material self is what everybody can see. Our conceptual self, on the other hand, has to do with perceptions of our identity. Because of our morbid fear of death, we strive to engage in activities that will keep our conceptual selves alive. We try to immortalize

ourselves by leaving legacies- our name on a building, charity, writing a book, etc.

According to Becker, almost everything there is today- government, art, and technological inventions- is propelled by the need to preserve our conceptual selves. Sometimes immortality endeavors of one group is at variance with another, resulting in conflicts and wars. Sometimes also, when our attempts at immortalizing ourselves lose significance, that crippling fear of death, which has been there all along, intensifies.

Those ideals you hold so dear- the ones that determine what you give a hoot about- are your immortality endeavors. Fear of eventually dying makes you want to care about too many things; do too many things so that you can temporarily forget you'll have to die someday. But it's when you care about fewer things that you've come to accept that you're not going to be here forever. It's only then that the chances of your becoming entitled are very slim. Better still, you have true power.

Truth is, much of the rat race that makes our lives so meaningless is fueled by our innate need to not die; to preserve our memories. We get involved in too many things and bother about too many things to keep from fizzling out, but we end up exactly where we don't want to. We need to come to terms with the fact that we all will die. When we accept that, it becomes easier to conserve our efforts for the things that truly matter, care about less things, and live better quality lives.

Our bodies naturally do not want to die. If you ever get as close to the edge of a cliff as ten feet, you'll experience your body giving out warning signals. Your feet become heavy and don't want to move and your skin tingles. These sensations become heightened as you move closer. Interestingly however, if you keep inching closer- going against your body's natural design- and get within just one step of plunging to your death, your senses become more heightened than ever and you'll become more aware than you've ever been.

When you completely accept the inevitability of death, you reach a realm in which the fear of dying no longer has a hold over you. You can ignore and say "No" to life's frivolities and messed-up values. You can choose good values and start giving a hoot about the right things. You can place more value on making the world a better place than making yourself unforgettable (ironically, the second is usually achieved when the first is a priority). You can stop feeling like the world owes you anything. You can choose the quality of problems you deal with. You can choose to suffer for the right things. You can fail without feeling like a failure. You can accept that uncertainty is not a bad thing. You can suffer, knowing the resilience it brings out in you. You can appreciate pain. You can stop giving a hoot about everything. You can live your best life.

90528127R00039

Made in the USA
San Bernardino, CA
11 October 2018